THE BOOK OF COLD MOUNTAIN

CAMERON KELLER SCOTT

BLUE LIGHT PRESS ✦ 1ST WORLD PUBLISHING

SAN FRANCISCO ✦ FAIRFIELD ✦ DELHI

WINNER OF THE 2016 BLUE LIGHT BOOK AWARD
THE BOOK OF COLD MOUNTAIN
Copyright ©2016 by Cameron Keller Scott

1ST WORLD LIBRARY
PO Box 2211
Fairfield, IA 52556
www.1stworldpublishing.com

BLUE LIGHT PRESS
www.bluelightpress.com
Email: bluelightpress@aol.com

BOOK & COVER DESIGN
Melanie Gendron
www.melaniegendron.com

COVER ART (Look Away and I Find You Within 1)
& INTERIOR ILLUSTRATIONS
Johanna Mueller
www.feverishart.com

FIRST EDITION

Library of Congress Control Number: 2016937088

ISBN 9781421837543

CONTENTS:

Acknowledgements

"Ants" in *Silk Road*

"Everyday we Navigate the Distance" in *River of Earth and Sky: Poems for the Twenty-First Century*

"Interlude with Ocho and Han Shan" first appeared in *The Book of Ocho* by AGS Press

"Late Summer Rain" in *Loam Magazine*

"Me, You, Pika" in *Clerestory Poetry Journal*

"Pilgrimage" from the anthology, *A Democracy of Poets*

"Premonition of Ashes, Premonition of Dust" in *Borderlands: Texas Poetry Review*

"Second Grace" in *Rhino*

"Scout Captions" in *The Fly Fish Journal, Volume Seven, Issue One*

"Songs from the Mountains" in *Rufous Press: Lush*

"Your Sentence is a River" and "Your Sentence is the Fall" in *Watershed Review*

"Your Sentence is a Midnight Swan" original and translated in *The Poem Café Quarterly*

Polar Bear Man

A Note About Cold Mountain

The manifestation of Han Shan in *The Book of Cold Mountain* first appeared in *The Book of Ocho*, a collection of poems written at 9,000 ft. while working as a fly-fishing guide and caretaking for a lymphomic cat. In Han Shan, a somewhat mad and whimsical poet, I found both detachment and love as I cared for Ocho. And although I tried on many other personas as I dealt with the grief of slowly losing Ocho (Rocky, Twilight Jesus, and Bad Blake just to name a few), it was Han Shan, toward the end of Ocho's life, that resonated with me most.

Interlude with Ocho and Han Shan

Every day the road gets more wash-boarded,
Ocho gets skinnier, I drive back and forth
from Cold Mountain to town and stand all day
in rivers, chewing gum incessantly, praising
cast after cast, come home and praise the cat,
go to work and praise the cast, come home.
Clients ask the way to Cold Mountain while
hip deep in currents; there's no thought to
carry them there, neither yes nor no as the sun
blazes down through swirling cottonwood seeds.

After *The Book of Ocho* was printed I left Cold Mountain for my current yearly winter migration to Oregon to work as a writer and teacher and attend artist residencies. It was at Playa, an artist residency outside of Summer Lake, Oregon, that a friend sent me Gary Snyder's *Cold Mountain Poems* and I sat down for the first time to fully immerse myself in the world of Han Shan. And as I returned to my own Cold Mountain for another summer of guiding, Gary Snyder's translation and Han Shan's voice once again came alive.

Cold Blooded

MIGRATION

In the middle of driving for two days without
radio through the great western desert
I sleep at the foot of a basin and range, retaining
no words, just heat. Un-noted. Un-selfied. Beneath
the light of a headlamp, lifting a lone water jug,
falling asleep beneath a waning moon.
To find that place inside that aches. To let
it grow smaller. To shrink. To eventually return
to a place of not thinking at all. This longing
to immerse in rivers. What of it? And now,
year after year, migration. How long? The things
we love most in this life are never ours. Why not?
Returning on the second day to Cold Mountain
I begin to climb. But why am I climbing? Han Shan,
I have traveled the loneliest highway in America,
but it is no lonelier than any place else.
Sometimes we seek connection and are granted.
Sometimes we seek disconnection and are granted.
Sometimes what is granted is not what we asked for.

Your Sentence is a Midnight Swan

It arrives at midnight. Feathers that smother.
A trembling heart. Fear for all the things that have left
as quickly as exhalations. An unrelaxable eye.
If you fall back asleep it is due to exhaustion.
Tomorrow is a river. You'll be standing next to
the holy ghosts of birds. Otters that swim
among stars. And if you part the moss
and rushes, you might find your own face peering
back at you before breaking into ten thousand moths.
Extra words will accumulate and take ownership
like rain. Tires will part water like four blackbirds
carrying a coffin. Time will slow down like molasses.
You are uncertain which part of your body
it will emerge from and when it will finally leave.
It will do no good to call it a midday swan.
To explain it away into rosehips and wild hops.
This huge bird so unlike an albatross. The lightning will
be unable to touch you. The sky will bend to your flight.

ALL HAN SHAN WANTS

Today, removing staples
with a pair of pliers
from a barn-wood window.
Tomorrow, anchor ice.
All Han Shan wants
is yesterday's water:
to write like a river,
fill each bend and cliff wall,
carry away sediment.
To become as streamlined
as a fish. To fall toward
the ocean. To make the great
migration, bank to bank,
past boats and barges.
To slip through dams and cities
to the sea. To push back
fin by fin into far reaching
branches, beginning to end,
end to beginning, and re-discover
each sentence as he goes.

PAINTING THE CEILING BLUE

Monday the scaffolding arrives.
The hardware store one block over
has everything Han Shan needs.
The air smells like fresh paint.
Tuesday his neck is a rock.
The brim of his hat captures the drips
of a newly birthed language.
He speaks in the rhythms
of a roller spreading paint.
Wednesday he fills in the last foot
of the thousand-square-foot
fifteen-foot-high ceiling, arm extended
as it has been for three days,
drinks a cold beer, and walks home.
No one else would take the job.
Rows of gold chandeliers stun
like earrings. Clothing displays hold
heads between hands. Up on
the ceiling a fresh coat of paint
slowly digests Han Shan's sadness.

The Way to Cold Mountain

i.

Scrub oak and sagebrush stretch unbroken
for as far as the eye can see. And beyond that?
A world. And beyond that? Another world.
Friends who have already departed and friends
who are soon to depart might someday return
while Han Shan roams the interior, finding sun
warmed rocks just right for napping. It is birds,
not cables, that stretch across horizons. It is bees,
not airplanes, which turn blossoms into honey.
When Han Shan walks back in the dark, three deer
run through the tall grass. No archway or road
to mark an entrance. No sleight of hand
or flick of switch welcomes Han Shan home.

ii.

Han Shan drives the empty highway for sixty
miles and passes one truck. Fingers lift from
steering wheel to wave. Through a small town
clothes flap from a clothesline next to a paint
peeled house. A gas station with faded lettering
and boarded windows. A trailer askew off
its foundation. Han Shan turns his head
and watches the truck's shadow knife down
the ribbon of road. Soon, gravel crunches beneath
wheels as he begins to climb. The town has no
name. The road remains nameless. Even tires
erase their tracks, forgetting which way to go.

COLD MOUNTAIN NEVER SLEEPS

Cold Mountain sits suspended above all dreams.
Travelers peer up, but stay on the path to the tea house
or brewery. My friend who writes from far away says
the weight of the mountain, the light of the mountain,
will follow you. Everything after apex is just descent.
But if you stay on the mountain your sleepless body
will eventually be swept away on the clouds.

Dust Both Ways

Three thousand vertical feet down Cold
Mountain. Three thousand vertical feet
back up. Han Shan waves to slow down
but I can't stop. Seven hundred fifty

thousand vertical feet by the end of summer.
Ground squirrels dodge tires, birds flit across
the windshield. Rabbits scatter. Coyotes
slip away. Errant deer leap fences. Fenced

cows which have broken out of their pasture
stand like brick walls. Cars dodge.
I roll down the road with the knucklebones
of sheep for tires. I am spinning, spinning,

like the hands of a clock. Name your wager.
Name your outcome. Each day more and more
dust hangs heavy in the air. Won't fall far.
Stuck to wheel wells, won't fall far at all.

THE MOMENT IS A RIVER PASSING

In the fury of a thousand fists
a listless storm of dandelion seeds.

The heart is a city on fire. The heat
is a pizza straight out of the oven.

Cellos and oboes are not organs
I would ever choose to transplant.

Even in the steady summer rain a fever
of instruments play over drops of water.

Little fish, big fish, doesn't really matter.
Only a drunk raven sleeps all day.

YOUR SENTENCE IS COLD MOUNTAIN

And Han Shan welcomes you. All summer
you scratch in the dirt and the wind and rain erases
your words. The husky from down the road
digs a hole in your favorite poem. Each day
you leave and burn like a small sun. At night
you return among the aspens; green, golden, bare.
Time passes like an arrow over the ridge. It is
all boiling water and steam until you spill your tea
across the counter in liquid arguments. Han Shan
laughs at your inability to read the leaves. Your
penmanship diminishes as the water evaporates.
You go to bed tired, every night tired on this
cold mountain you have been climbing, climbing
into the star tipped sky, but heaven is just like any
other word. When the world sees poets it says
we are all crazy, not much to look at, dressed
in rags and the personas of four dozen animals.
What I say is you cannot skip out on your sentence
in good conscience. It will eat you from the inside.
If Cold Mountain calls, you must go. They say it's
a foolish dream. What dream isn't? My home was
on Cold Mountain from the start. Only from far away
can the world finally sink deep into your bones
and come out like five shadows, a storm cloud, pricks
of sleet blossoming on your raw flesh like daisies.

Year of the Horse

Han Shan passes through a grove of spruce.
Squirrels chitter and scold. Maybe human-less
silence is more humane. Maybe prefers fire
curled around kettle to pixels, boiling water
to cables. Stars go blue. Seas go red. Eyes go
white like flags, flutter from heaven as feathers.
Han Shan adjusts the delicate positioning
of his cot between bear and bobcat. Falls asleep
as fingers dip into the mouth of a mountain lion.
Chipmunks disappear. One by one, roots up-
rooted. Tunnels dug. Nests built. Last year
is no longer this year. This year seems like
last year anyway. Nettle stew tastes the same.
A new wooden spoon to carve. Broken bowls
to mend. But frozen ideas, swaddled in blankets
of sunlight, melt as Han Shan re-emerges, his
bowed neck, a ridge. Beneath spongy loam
the boulders of his hands cup water. Washing
his face, Han Shan appears a madman, re-emerges
as wet rivulets. In the Happy Valley below,
what is a lie, what passes for truth? On Cold
Mountain, Han Shan hides everything but his face.

COLD MOUNTAIN C.R.E.A.M.

If one morning Han Shan woke up from Wu'Tang
I would float away from Cold Mountain as a dream.
Accept impoverishment without being impoverished.
Sustain the insatiable. These things that steal, also steal
from us. The hand that grips the stock cannot be the right
hand or wrong hand. Ol' Dirty knew this, all hands are
human, hungry. We haven't yet told ourselves how to be
full, to accept our lives as nothing and everything. Face
the darkness of a barrel, and see light there instead.

First Friday in the Happy Valley

Some days the world sweeps away death,
the clinking of bells, a bone flute. Some days
ignorance loses. There is dancing. But after
ten thirty tacos, night deflates. Drunken ninjas
are funny, sad clowns weep. The streets become
a carnival without music. When the lighthearted
have left it is also time to leave. Tuck the kazoo
into my pocket and depart back through sober lines
of aspen trunks. The journey up Cold Mountain
is like a dream. Tires float over potholes and rocks,
foot never lets off the gas, except for a porcupine,
just after midnight, wandering up the road.

Scout, Captions

Scout runs in circles as I ring out my wet clothes
and spill water from my waders.
Scout rolls in the dead carcasses of kokanee salmon
and walks by Brooke causing her to gag.
Scout watches from shore, sprawled in poison oak.
Scout smells a cougar.
Scout shreds the pheasant skin on the fly tying table.
Scout spends all day eating grasshoppers.
shatters Pyrex shepherd's pie pan from counter,
drags deer femur through dog door,
catches a ground squirrel mid-sprint
and drops it at my feet.
Scout, what secrets do mayflies have
who travel on the backs of clouds?
Scout sits with her head between her paws
while customers gaze
at the one hundred and two pound king salmon
above the cash register asking if it is real.
Scout sells the mule deer salt and pepper shakers
to a woman from Lubbock, Texas.
Scout takes the waffle iron on vacation.
Scout fixes the hole in the shower tile
and pulls out the rotten drywall.
Scout gets paid under the table.
Scout, what of light as it runs low,
what of darkness as it presses in?
Scout sprawled on the floor
like Elvis's immobile hips.
Scout posed like Marylyn's dress that no longer lifts.
Scout eats rat poison and lives.
Scout holds the world together
with her soft brown fur.

Scout plunges into runoff
and disappears around the bend.
Scout laps the treble of water
running over broken slate.
Scout stares into the base of deep blue pools.
Scout pukes up the entrails in the middle of the night.
Scout, what of all these rivers
that tumble toward the silver sea?

SECOND GRACE

Holding your body must be a poem
because I have not written a poem in weeks.

As the white Chevy Silverado cuts me off from behind
and the pale face staring out the window shoots me the finger
I try to calm down which also takes place of a poem.

As does the uneven green grass of the front yard which has
instantaneously grown inches in the past week,
the dandelions which spread their arms trying to
hold back the grass and a long silver implement
with a wooden handle to pop them deep at the roots.

There is no end to the things that can be replaced; dead flesh
by crystal, wood by rock. Or an old black truck
at the dealership. Soon I will leave and a third grace
will replace the second. Then a fourth.

As the summer unfolds away from you, grace in place
of grace, not holding your body will be the poem
I write over and over, a hundred times in a hundred
different ways.

Sweat and sunscreen in the corners of my eyes.
A river pushing at my legs.

Heavy Orange Moon

As he sleeps, Han Shan rises over open country.
Deserts. Ranges of mountains. Grasslands.
On top of Cold Mountain, Han Shan can look
down and see his own reflection. A thousand
thousand mirrorings. Light bounces and lays down
a pathway to his feet. The moon whispers
to Han Shan. Light spills out of his eyes.
Even hidden on the other side of the world,
the moon pulls at Han Shan so hard he wants
to yip and snarl. Full of old songs, Han Shan
knows the meanings, but none of the words.

Through Cold Mountain

When time flows away and cuts into sleep and Sappho
has left from Newark and Newark is a starting point,
but not a place I have ever been, in those pixels on
the screen, *N E W A R K: On Time*, maybe, just maybe,
she will step from plane to tarmac, surrounded by
mountains and staring at Cold Mountain decide to stay
for a while somewhere up the twists and turns of
the windy road. And before she leaves will tell me
she loves most these things: amber scales of daylight, purple
chandeliers of dusk, columbines billowing in afternoon sun.

After Sappho, Rumi

The glass was formed at the hands of the glass blower.
A rounded container the light spills through.
My clumsy hand reaches into darkness,
knocks the glass onto the concrete floor.
I smashed the glass, but did not fall anywhere.
The glass blower was long gone, though I was still filled
with heat. Small shards stuck in my bare feet.
Where time flows backward glass dislodges from flesh.
Back into form, glass. Back into container, water.
Hand retreats. Body returns to bed. But the dream
cannot reverse. The one where I am falling headlong
into the soft flesh of desire. Something has gone
wrong. The glassblower formed my heart like a delicate
egg. The thing meant to hatch becomes a mess.
A collapsing mass of energy entire planets cannot fill.

Han Shan Shatters the Glass

Call upon the glassblower, heat from the belly of
the earth, molten, long rod, spear, glowing fire, astral arc.
This glass out of the kiln glows red or orange or white
then cools into color. The way light catches and cuts,
swings, elongates. Here I was alive, enacted upon by some
force. A clumsy hand. Unseeing eyes. Of energy
other than fire. To hold the glass. To heat and watch
a thousand thousand grains shift alive, to call
by any other name that which hallows out a soul.
If we are the energy that creates certain things
with glass, love cools, cracks cannot repair, form cannot
recover. I heard the way to Cold Mountain was to walk
into the molten sun until you hear the caged atom call.
I was there when the glassblower shaped this shattered
thing. How the hidden flame burns, how it might shape us,
but never once we are broken, be used to reshape us again.

The Bull

In the green meadow below Cold
Mountain it runs, muscles in its shoulders
thick as velvet billows. Hidden from
the Happy Valley, it protects pasture
while horns and back taper down into
something lithe and graceful. What kind
of matador slowly slices and bleeds
with sleight of hand and steel? The only
kind of matador there is. And who shall feel
compelled to run the fields of endless
summer with bulls charging from behind?
Han Shan feels compelled. What does it
mean anymore to be Han Shan? Everyday
Han Shan jumps the fence and makes
his way to the river. In each pool, a pasture.
In one hand, a long slender lance.
In the other, the inevitable red flag.

ADRIFT IN THE VALLEY OF HAN SHAN

After each day adrift in the pulse of the valley
forty thousand thieves have ransacked the caravan
and I return weary and sad. Cold Mountain sits
to the side like a cloud. Wind instead of highway.
Humming birds instead of hominids. A choice
to steal or have everything stolen. Beggar. Thief.
Han Shan, is it possible to un-predict reason?
Questions may be answered or unanswered, thoughts
finished or unfinished, but what does the sky care
if it goes in circles? Does passion affect the instability
of air? Does spinning earth attempt cover from
insatiable sun? Snow sits heavy on the ridge,
spring cannot get here fast enough, but isn't it
already spring in the Happy Valley below?

Everyday We Navigate the Distance

Aspen leaves in the wind,
fingers tapping the table—

How can you know for certain
just by the familiar sound a thought makes,
breaking through branches?

At the sound of your name,
a hint of salt and mesquite.

After dusk, the crunch and sweep
of footsteps like names swept away.

If I said pine. If I said sage. If I dressed
in red clay, with charcoal, with ashes,
would your name come back to me?

If I balanced fourteen stones
through which I could still see the sky,
would your name continue to haunt me
in this kingdom of light?

Me, You, Pika

In the rosehips, in the scree.
Great big ears, small furry body.

I could fit this endangered thing in my hands
and it would struggle.

I could fit this wild thing in my hands,
heart beating too fast.

Still, I'm ready with steel leg bands and plastic ear tags.
I'm ready to stuff it in my jacket pocket,
lined with loam and grass.

Hunting with my hands I've forgotten about the big looming shape
of my body. I've forgotten about the creek

which tumbles over the moraine's lip
and disappears beneath boulders.

I search the fading light in the direction of the pika's shrill whistle.

This is what I dream about, in my dream,
late at night in the high alpine cirque.

The whole world encroaches on me, you, and the pika. There is only one
of each of us. Just one of each of us left,
and I'm out of my mind to hold it
in my hands.

Han Shan Dreams of Birds

When you call there is still some arctic light left
in a foundering pocket of sky. I have a mouse clutched
in my talons and a gull chasing me from behind.
On the edge of marsh, sandhill cranes and geese
bicker with each other, ducks get caught in the fray.
You call again, and I answer. You're on the shed roof,
I'm on the fence post. Hearing you, it is everything
to know the dusk has given us back from the arms
of windmills, the headlights of oncoming cars.

WAKING UP WITH HAN SHAN

When you live on Cold Mountain your ego is punctured.
All of your hot air goes out as the morning rushes in.
You must forget about yourself and immerse in the world
that moves around you. How awful the bee sting, how
painful the thorn in the foot. How artful the souls of your feet
when they thicken, and your hands, which birth fire
when you finally notice the honeycomb, reachable in the tree.

Your Sentence is Night

Your sentence is as encompassing as
the night. Your sentence is soft blue
light, a neon highlight, a glowing wrist-
watch. Your sentience a handful of
spruce. Your night wanderings like
geese. Where coyotes weep, city lights
cheapen the stars. At night, cars flood
empty corridors and deer thought
dead in the ditch, scratch at the door
to the underworld, lift the catch,
and escape. Unable to sleep, your
sentence is a senseless glower. Watts,
kilowatts, one thousand torches
caught in this bright, relentless pull.

PREMONITION OF ASHES, PREMONITION OF DUST

i.   Premonition of Ashes

Ashes of cedar. Ashes of grace.
Subterranean ashes. Homesick
fire, blowing in the blood.
This brief and naked burning
brought to its graceless knees.
Still down in the trenches. Fall-
out like isotopes dispersed in so
many parts per million. Where what
makes us dirty also makes us clean.

ii.   Premonition of Dust

Dust of sandstone. Dust of faith.
Ground down. Dander. Pollen.
Mites and the heavy metals
of meteorites. Organic or inert,
crystalline viral shards, hauntings,
spooks. Dust to dust, aflame
in the atmosphere catching last
of sun. Dinosaurs. Light
enough to wander air currents.
In each flake of snow, a seed.

HAN SHAN DEPARTS COLD MOUNTAIN

The dog barks. A door shuts. Gravel crunches
under tires. A long cloud of dust rises from
the dirt road, a descent of lifetimes takes
minutes. There is a brown-leafed plant
in the corner and dog shit on the concrete floor.
Milk has gone bad. Dressing's past due.
Air so dry red eyes leak constant tears.
Pair of holey running shoes left on the porch.
From now on Han Shan will bathe and oil
his own feet. No one will take him seriously.
Like the moon. Or dusk. A coyote yips.
And yips again. Yipee kayayayay-eeeeyah.
Eeeeeeyah. Two cougar cubs run off the road
at midnight, as a black truck hurtles past.

A Vision of Han Shan as Poet

On Cold Mountain at dusk
Han Shan sits in a cathedral of aspen.
Head tilted up in what must be

reverence but might also be called
surprise. He has chosen to become
a columbine. There in the thicket

alert and reverent as a bear. When
Han Shan re-enters the human world,
he carries in the smell of puffball

mushrooms growing in patches of
dandelions, a carpet of needles
and squirrel chewed cones, aspen leaves

which flutter like litanies to the sun,
green and rich with chloroform.
On the extensions of those prayers

Cold Mountain will turn golden, then
white and barren, then green again.
So rich and full of imagination while also

moving toward absentia, Han Shan lives
among these groves. In this way he sheds
poems like golden leaves before winter.

The Monks of Freezy Mountain

One dances for five hours and drives home in the dark.
One becomes like a heap of blossoms.
One smiles as if under water, only visible if undisturbed.

VIRGINIA WOOLF VISITS COLD MOUNTAIN

In the novel, Mrs. Dalloway said she would buy
the flowers herself. But they are growing wild
on Cold Mountain's slope, there for anyone who
makes the climb. Virginia, was there ever

a time when we were unafraid to choose our
own destinies? When life was simple as a
mountain's silhouette against openly darkening
sky? So many things seem filled with the intent

to be lost. And it is at dusk when I call upon you.
And at dusk you receive me. For the mountain to
emerge from the darkness it takes our hands
and feet to feel our way through bone white groves.

Our ears and mouths to move through dark hollows.
To seek resuscitation, to revive words, to revive all
the hours we know we lost but are unable to remember;
when and where each went missing, or for how long.

Cold Mountain Way

Han Shan is a grain of sand. How many
grains of sand is Han Shan? What we carry
with us today drops from us tomorrow.
Han Shan is one grain of sand among
many. He watches grasshoppers spring
from the front of his footsteps as he walks
down the path to the river. More sand
in this world than Han Shan's worth.
Where the tracks of yesterday's visitors
tell the story of each grain's passing.

Van Morrison Visits Cold Mountain

And they whisper secrets about trees
having fallen across currents, stripped
of bark, silver in the sunlight, windfall
collecting cased caddis and midges. Into
the softening evening they thrum.
Into the darkness. Into the absolute darkness
of rain so heavy it becomes a flood,
a giant river, an all-enveloping music. In the very
darkness of life. In the absolute dark
the trees extract themselves and wander down
the trail. Sodden travelers seeking shelter
in the Happy Valley like everyone else.
When Van Morrison leaves he passes tree
after tree heading down as mist toward a fire.
Time parts the way water parts around a rock;
smoothing it, moving it, suddenly lifting it.
All along the path to Cold Mountain is music.

COLD MOUNTAIN VARIATIONS

In some versions Han Shan is driven
away by hunger but returns in the fall
to hibernate. Perhaps he is gluttonous.
Or more finely adapted to famine.
In other versions he never leaves.
Driven to wake up at dawn to watch
first light break across ridge and slant
through aspen. Bull of the lilies.
Goldilocks of the broken bells. Some-
times Han Shan talks to Emily Dickinson.
Could stay on Cold Mountain for years
having bearlike conversations with dirt.
The brief blossoming of non-native
poppies. The longer grief of columbine.

Songs from the Mountains

I.

Thunderstorm:
If it strikes on Hell Roaring Ridge
it strikes again on the Frying Pan.

Han Shan is a poet and a madman.
Have you seen him? Does he
fly low in the headlights like an owl
up the corridor of the rock rutted road?

II.

Under a bare sky
these endless days of summer.

Under storm
these endless days of summer.

Beneath the sky, these endless days.

III.

When there was an upstream wind, I forward rowed.
It was never love, just some odd current.

IV.

Ebbs and currents carry us
with the weight of something larger
pressing against our driftwood bones.

V.

I can't tell you what pushes me
step after step, ascending above tree line.

It wasn't the sight of two ptarmigan,
one which flew over stunted spruce,
the other, browning to white, which sang
on the granite dome above the lake.

But it might have been the marmot
which made off with my bag of trail mix
ducking into its dry dirt den
two hundred yards up the steep ridge.

VI.

Skip me across the universe and let me sink
for I am flat and smooth and whistle
through the air, spinning off the water
that wore me smooth, my only chance at love.

VII.

So what if a bear breaks in and eats
all the dog food. Buy more dog food.

VIII.

And who, if I ordered another beer,
would hear me softly singing
with my head resting against the wall
above the urinal.

IX.

Of the wind through aspens which is never still.
Of the water that slips over rocky shelves in thin braids,
running down windows in thunderstorms.
Both are woven together like strands of rug.

X.

A puffball mushroom bigger than two fists,
a bushel of nettles tied with twine.
All I can think of as we return to the truck
is won't you be mine?

XI.

Two hundred yards away I can hear the river
through thick brush. Dusk is an inlet
which thickens like fog.

XII.

Even if the summer suddenly came back to life
it would be like a dry fly drowning
or nymphs dragging across the surface of the water
until one of them gets smacked by a trout.

Which is surprisingly good.
Dragging across the surface of the water
and getting smacked by a trout.

XIII.

Before there were rivers
Han Shan fished
the black nothingness of space.

Han Shan's Eyes

In the morning when my eyes are too tired
to think about the day ahead I let them
wander off as if on a walk. With a pillow
over my head or t-shirt wrapped around
my face like a bandanna, I'm never sure where
they go. Minutes pass until the alarm brings
them back into focus. Some mornings how
delicious to let them slip away for whole
hours. They come back sleek as otters from
the river. This morning they flew open thirty
minutes before the alarm. Aren't you tired?
I ask them. Unable to focus they chew through
bed sheets and smash dishes. My bad eyes
have lives of their own. Two milky galaxies.
Two black bats. Two yellow peonies
thrusting their heads toward a burning sun.

FISHMONGER

A chipmunk scampers along the top of
a garden wall where daisies push toward
the sun and the sun pushes across the sky
blazing, ablaze, blue with a point so bright
it burns. Today is the day of the town fair
where each resident of the Happy Valley
celebrates Cold Mountain as Cold Mountain
presses its ear against the heavy wooden door
that separates the inside from outside.
Hula hoops, jam bands, Indian food and beer.
Leather workers. Smithies. Glass blowers.
When the fair comes to town almost everyone
pauses and inhales except for Han Shan
who must go to the river to gather fish. Today
is like every other. When Han Shan closes
his eyes, he opens them and it is already
morning. A morning still enough to embrace.
Han Shan is inside Cold Mountain. Cold Mountain
is inside Han Shan. When Han Shan goes to gather
fish, he carries Cold Mountain inside, untouchable.

When Pine Martens Become a Daily Sighting

First it was bears, chewing on the window-
sill trying to break into the kitchen. Then
it was foxes and coyotes slipping through
fences. But now, five times in six days,
pine martens dart in and out of bank
rocks and current. Framed by red sandstone
and patches of white daisies leaning out
over the water. Their sleek bodies remind me
of corvettes. Needle sharp teeth and claws
that shred. Invader of will. And for a moment
I want to be a small fish held to a marten's
chest, spinning through the current, all
the life going out of me. All summer, out lasting
rain, out lasting sun, outlasting wind. Of all
the animals who make Cold Mountain home,
which have much to say about hunger? Which
will tell you they are ready to sleep? Which
have much to say about anything at all?

Han Shan and Squirrel

When there's nothing left to say I want to be the one
to sweep away this year's pine needles
lift two handfuls of dirt
and chitter like a mad squirrel.
This is the world I'm from talking to other worlds.
Uprooting soma soya shad shah
and feasting upon them in the sun rust afternoon.
Let me break apart the earth and offer
the ability to affect the respiratory system
of clouds. Let me call upon the upland meadows
and ravines of the mountains
that inhabit the bitter roots of my soul and wild
craft out of this nothingness amp amah a map.
To open continually like the dawn doe dark
and draw into each breath heath fell moor.
Gather unreasonable words from each tree
on the hillside and when I am done
travel the world like a beggar with an empty bowl.

COLD MOUNTAIN'S SILENCE

Before I go to work for the fiftieth
day in a row I wanted to become Cold
Mountain. To unmake the mundane.
To seek forgiveness for an appetite
that cannot be satiated. The harder
I work the more hungry I become the
more I want to lose myself in the tramp-
lings of daisies and arrive homeless
on Cold Mountain's steppes. But given
enough time, even Cold Mountain
will change. For all of the most hidden
songs to be sung, silence must be broken.

Your Sentence is a Garden of Daisies

And the animal that bedded down in them.
The deer that suddenly springs away. The bear
who stands up on hind legs and does not.

Your Sentence is a Gravy Train

The price of chicken fried steak is gravy.
As is the boat, which came across the shining sea.
The cow may not think highly of the cook.
Nor natives of the newly minted inhabitants.
But gravy covers history and biscuits alike.
As we grow up each of us must ask ourselves
if we can stomach it. And some of us
will not be able to stand to be smothered
in so much. We pray for absence. Abstinence.
And still gravy falls like manna from heaven.
For the one who died for the sins of our arteries;
the virgin waitress Mary, the chef Jose.

Late Summer Rain

Twilight Jesus shows up soaking wet on the doorstep.
I am the coyote who ran beneath your truck yesterday
then disappeared into the dripping wet world.
Too tired to question. Too hungry for mystery.
For two days the daisies crumple on their stems.
Rain gutters sing of silence and sorrow. The bees
stay inside the hive beneath the eves. Cold Mountain
is shrouded in mist. As if all the world has melted.
Han Shan does not have to travel far to discover things
he cannot readily see. Part of the world is dying.
Part of the world is drowning. Part of the world will be
even greener and more vibrant than it was before.

ANTS

I.   Twilight Jesus and the Ants

Beneath the rain the quiet hill
glistens in the heat of sun a mass
alight a swarm of amber appendages
black carapaces sleek as fiberglass red
as sides of butchered beef jalapeno
pinchers Twilight Jesus on his last day
prayed to be carried away and so it was
when his heart finally squeezed shut
a moving river appeared from
the open window shook the carpets
cleaned his bones to perfection
as he ascended in the glory of ants.

II.   Country Singer w/Ants

A dog lays down too close a truck
breaks down too often too few
enter the woodpile and ever emerge
the queen holds equation after equation
in her abdomen the sun rises and falls
one ant is no ant no ego to fall prey to
for it is ants who praise dead grasshoppers
and ants who exalt in spilled soda
and bread crumbs and country singers
who spend all afternoon passed out
on the lawn crawled on crawled over
crawled into each day preparing for
that emptiness in the world called winter.

COLD MOUNTAIN FORGERY

Why do I leave so fast each day? All I want
sits above tree line. What can I quit
that I'm not already abandoning?
Somewhere between the earth and sky
is a counterfeit. Each day the river becomes
more difficult a forgery. I hold it up
to the light, looking for watermarks.

OUTLIER

When I close my eyes to dream at night
I dream of people fishing. "That was
a big one" they say, turning to me.
Sometimes all that matters is a few fish
in the net. Sometimes just one big fish.
"How do you move so fast through currents?"
they ask. *Ten thousand hours. I have slept
next to rivers more nights than I can recall.
I have not slept at all.* Sometimes nothing
is good enough. Sometimes I have to be
careful about receiving too much praise.
Too many nights next door at the bar. Too
many orders of wings and beer. All the fish
they lose. All the fish they catch. All the hours
spent standing in rivers. When I close my eyes,
how close we feel, how distant we become.

THREE-HOUR TOUR

When a trout rises for a dry fly
slowly toward the light
mouth first
how does it sometimes
end up with the fly
stuck in its ass?
Life is not glamorous.
Some days a pilgrimage
made on our knees.
Today all the flies ended up
in the mouths
of all the biggest trout.
I should fall asleep grateful.
Laughter and cigar smoke
blowing in the wind.
But I keep looking at the road.
And wonder when my life
draws close to closing
what kind of meaning
these moments will carry.

Your Sentence is to Wake

As Han Shan crosses the threshold
of dreams. To contend with
lost fish. If you were a patron saint,
and you are not, but if you were,
you'd be the patron saint of undoing
tangles, of how to smooth away
defeat, create acceptance. To walk
through and point out fish belly up
in the back eddy. To show certainty
but to know there is none. To invoke
prayer with every cast and with
every step become less and less
certain. Your patron saint is
Han Shan. Cold Mountain your
sanctuary. You are a cloud in the sky.

What is Left in August

Each day I wake up and eat a bowl
of cereal, put ice in the cooler, and drive
down Cold Mountain to stand in rivers.
Today's fish are the same as yesterday's,
but today's fish refuse to eat. Still, we
stand in a river trying to catch something
that does not want to be caught. August
bows. I bow. The rainbow leaps into the air
before spitting the hook. Sometimes rejection
is the thing we need most. When everything
is so full it hurts. As it hurts to finally
understand what it means to be
standing in a river so close to the divine.

PREMONITION

Even on Cold Mountain
steel disassembles. Iron
weakens. Diamonds
dropped into liquid oxygen
burn. Han Shan sits at
a dice game with Coyote.
"I know who you are,"
says Han Shan. "Even the
parts of the universe
which are illusion
reveal the dream itself."

COLD MOUNTAIN'S LIGHT

The mountain at night is a dark body.
The universe is there or not there;
written in a language of far off lights.
The sun is the star who birthed the light
that birthed the light that birthed my
mother and father. From Cold
Mountain, the chaos of stars, and what
came before. There is no mistake, but
often we are mistaken. How long our
light will travel, and what the destination.

NOSTALGIA

Winter breaks suddenly like a hare from beneath sprung sagebrush
and the soft ground, after weeks of falling leaves and rain
holds ice, frozen rivulets of water, and snow. I want to make a break
for it, too. From this modern human world of global warming
and jihad, but am afraid of running right into coyote's open mouth
while looking over my shoulder. Even as I stop,
the sun cold against my face, I miss how the sun used to be.

First Snow

When gods are small, when gods are humble,
when sunlight reaches the earth after days of rain,
when flowers stand up straight again
and clouds don't wander lost along the edges
of mountains. Have you remembered to
stock the woodpile? Have you remembered
extra candles, days when light is extinguished?
Today's sun is not tomorrow's. Bit by bit
a few more animals begin to hibernate, crawl
beneath the earth and disappear. Soon
the only animals left will be winter, sweeping
before it newly fallen snow, and sleep,
which will come in fits and storms. What does
Han Shan dream if he remembers to dream at all?
What will he call this long, tired, forgetfulness?
From spring to solstice all the small and hum-
ble gods gather. When the world is easy.
When the animals within us are still beautiful,
and the earth opens up to welcome us home.

Your Sentence is the River

The way each word carries past.
The way each day carries. Your sentence
is to sit on red sandstone and mossy rocks
and feel the words and days press against
your submerged feet. Old salt knows
the pull of water, fathoms deep, but
snowmelt knows the push. To begin is
to stand in the flow. To end is to push off.
Everything carried downstream is flotsam.
Each wreckage that washes in from the sea
stranded on the river's great delta. Barges.
Dirges. The way each singer carries
the ashes of the dead. There is no
underworld, there are only flowers
that spring up from the soil.

Your Sentence is the Fall

Again, snow on the peaks. Again, yellow leaves
find their way from branches into the river,
drift deeper and deeper, with less and less light.
Wake up from work to find summer's passing
and in resignation return to winter. If there
is anticipation for everything, looking forward,
why do some of us burrow like velvety moles
only to emerge in the perfection of spring?
Is it the way we are meant to worship, when
the earth is soft and food is frequent, when
everything is tender then the tenderest of us
emerge in reverence? Bears did not always
hibernate like bears. Blubinous balls of muscle,
fur and fat. Each a small sun. Each as terrible
as summer itself. But instead were more slender
like wolves. Less solitaire. Roamed in packs. Were
once as small as squirrels and as frequent. It is
one thing to say you know winter. And another
to live through winter after winter, present
through squall and swale. A living ice. Ever
present hunger, body itself a storm.
Even the sea has its seasons of light. Even
the mole will emerge and offer its tenderest
parts to the coyote or hawk. Even then there
is a difference between the name and the thing.
To be part of the world or the world itself.

Your Sentence is Ending

Strike out every single I from the text. Leave no link.
Trace no pleasure. Ignore vegetables and wander some other
cellular avenue. Exist out of time and not be bothered. Buy
a scarf. Be forgotten and by some grace forget yourself
but not a warm winter coat. Embody the word. Re-learn
what it means to enjamb. Immolate the word. Bury
a freezer. Use a snow bank. Rediscover earth and find out
it is red. Full of genocidal blossoms. Vanitas. Talk yourself
through a vow of silence. Reweave the loom. Use a game
camera to capture the night movements of your neighbors.
Wilt in large green piles. Associate phrase with stem. Slender
with loss. Bird with island. Climb into winter with only a box
of matches when there are too few suns to span the sky.

HAN SHAN, READY TO CROSS

Eventually there will be no spaces to inhabit.
No rabbits in the hutch. No birds in the next.
Time will sweep before it like newly fallen snow.
Will we have chance start us anew, a fresh, again,
to become picked or unpicked, the last apple
hanging from the branch after harvest? What
will become of us? Surely we are replaceable.
Must embrace impermanence. Be like
flowers. In the vase. On the vanity. Will we
be devoured by time? Of course we might
find a way to live forever, like stardust.
Pieces of other things. Even less concerned
with reading Whitman or inhabited by Howl
the way deer hanging out by the highway some-
times disintegrate when they step into the light.

The Fisher King

What's life, if not a wound, surely
something similar to water slipping
over stones. A place where
all the braids deepen into one
long run with an even seam
of current and some rocks to break
the flow. In the end, the river is
everything, and everything the river.

Pilgrimage

After dark, driving blind and drifting on 82
as Mt. Sopris shifts positions, clouds shift,
the river grade rises and wraps around corners.
I am a body in motion, the first one toward heaven.
I am a body at rest, a second palming of death.
A seat within a seat, closest to weary, cousin
to the midnight bus. Vehicles nod in succession.
The snow that blows sideways, sticks sideways.
The river that falls like a silver fish in the snow,
road sign to the soul, finds a path home each night
as the canyon opens up and swallows it whole.

YOUR FINAL SENTENCE

Grace does not come easy, not from
four months being immersed in rivers
or next door at the bar drinking Coors light.

Not a hundred and twenty lonely rides home
or the entire life of an aspen leaf from green
bud to yellow-brown carpet on forest floor.

Han Shan walks forty days and forty nights
in different directions and ends up in the same
place. None of him know how this happens.

"Here we are," says Han Shan, "absolved
of all our fish." "Yes," says Han Shan,
"and a few golden stems of grass have shot

their way out from winter's grasp like a rabbit
out from under the talons of a hawk."
"But," adds Han Shan, "isn't it winter we've
been looking forward to all along?"

Walking into Winter

Tell me everything you know about bones
as the snow accumulates and mountains
disappear from this steep sided valley

where aspen rise like coral, black ravens,
yellow leaves, and rigs slowly drive by in 4WD
trailers empty or full of elk, this road

where tires have churned thick mud
which smells of cows, and left a mohawk
of white. Each step I walk over hoof prints

in an ocean of sagebrush and scrub oak
my sacrament of love and fallen leaves,
my sacrament of moving, moving slowly,

as slowly into the breath of snow and wind
in my winter coat as one who knows it
is nearly time to say goodbye.

Spirit Bear

About the Author

Cameron Keller Scott graduated from the University of Arizona with an MFA in poetry. Most recently he has worked for *Chiloquin Visions in Progress* and *Fishtrap* as a writer in residence, as well as helping to implement Fishtrap Story Lab (www.fishtrap.org). His freelance work has appeared in *High Country News*, *The Drake*, *The Fly Fish Journal*, and *The Ski Journal* and he currently writes an outdoor column called Steelhead Nation for the *La Grande Observer*. He is also the author of *The Book of Ocho* and an editor for *A Democracy of Poets*, a finalist in the Colorado Book Awards.

CPSIA information can be obtained
at www.ICGtesting.com
Printed in the USA
BVOW08s2239150118

505283BV00004B/487/P